Tales of Iran 2

Feridon Rashidi

Published by New Generation Publishing in 2015

First Edition

www.newgeneration-publishing.com

New Generation Publishing

To Jane
with all my love and gratitude

Contents

Game Over

After kicking our shabby rubber ball around in the dust, we were sitting in the shade of a wall, lost in our daydreams. The lane was baking in the late afternoon sun. Soon a sickly-looking cockerel with a bald neck and tattered feathers hopped out of the hovel opposite, followed by a clutch of hens. No sooner outside than they began pecking at the dung and filth in the dusty patch in front of the door, clucking noisily. They vied with one another to get the attention of the cockerel, which strutted among them with its neck upright, keeping a sharp eye on the hens, as if it was still healthy and in control. The drowsy quiet of the village was every now and then shattered by a peasant, who walked behind his donkey, which was overburdened with sheaves of wheat, cursing and jabbing its backside with a stick, the point of which was studded with a nail.

All of a sudden, a skinny donkey with scabrous skin was pushed outside the hovel, followed by a limping, worn-out peasant. From the neighbouring hovel another man, a scythe slung on his shoulder, appeared. I heard the worn-out peasant say to him, "Seeing my mother like that breaks my heart."

Prodding their donkeys, the two men headed towards the fields outside the village. A cool breeze began to blow through the lane, so we got up and went on playing with our ball. As dusk neared, the game became more and more exciting as we were not able to see the ball easily in the twilight. At one stage some of us were looking for the ball which we could not find anywhere. Then one of the boys, who enjoyed playing pranks on us, stopped and extracted the ball from inside his shirt. "Found it! Found it!" he shouted. We all laughed and went on playing.

Upon hearing some angry shouts, we stopped and looked about, peering into the half-darkness to see who it was. I saw a phantom-like form trotting towards us, yelling. I made out the worn-out peasant, who was brandishing his stick.

"Don't you know, you godless urchins, that my mother is very ill and dying?" I heard him shout as he came closer to us. "At this time of day she needs to rest and you're making a racket, chasing after your damned ball."

There was something in his anguished voice that forced us to stand still and listen to him with our eyes lowered.

"I tell you what I'm going to do this time," the peasant went on. "I'm going to take your ball away from you as a punishment for your inconsiderate behaviour."

"But we only have this ball to play with," I mumbled, hugging the ball, which I had picked up. "If you take it away, how are we supposed to play without a ball?"

"Yeh, yeh, Amir's right." A chorus of my friends' voices backed me up.

"But all that is left me in this world is my mother," said the peasant, now a little calmer.

My friends looked at me. I understood the meaning in their looks. Reluctantly, I took a few steps towards the peasant and handed the ball to him without saying a word.

*

The morning after, around noon, as I was squatting on the edge of the brook outside our house, splashing handfuls of water on my face, I heard my auntie talking about the worn-out peasant to one of the women from the neighbourhood.

"Have you heard that poor Hajar's health is getting worse?" my auntie asked, dipping some linen into the water.

"Yes, I heard about it when I was at the spring source," replied the other woman, wringing a wet shirt in hands the colour of salmon flesh.

"Do you know what made it worse?" my auntie asked, lifting up the dripping linen.

"No, I don't," replied the other woman.

"Haven't you heard about that miracle-maker who's come to Ahmadabaad?"

"You mean the holy mollah?"

"That's the one."

"Yes, he's the talk of the village," said the other woman, slapping a shirt against a large stone on the edge of the brook. "What about him?"

"Following the example of many good sons who want to find a cure for their mothers, Safarali Cholagh took his mother to Ahmadabaad to be cured by the saintly mollah."

"How on earth did he take her there?"

"He carried her on his back."

"On his back!" the other woman almost cried out. "All the way to Ahmadabaad! Why didn't he take her on his donkey?"

“Haven’t you seen the donkey?” my auntie asked, placing the linen in a tin tub. “It’s on its last legs. Carrying all those heavy burdens all its life has bowed its back. The weight of the old woman would’ve broken it for good. All Safarali Cholagh has in this world are his mother, the donkey, a skinny cockerel, and a handful of aging hens.”

“So what happened to her in Ahmadabad?”

“Hearing about the saintly healer,” my auntie said, “all the cripples, idiots, and hopelessly sick folk walked, crawled, or were carried on donkeys to Ahmadabaad.”

“Did the he manage to cure the sick woman?”

“*Aey baba*, what cure?” My auntie sighed. “There was such a crush of people stampeding on each other that the old woman fell off Safarali’s back and was trampled by the mob who all desperately wanted to be healed of their incurable illnesses.”

My friends and I had no choice but to wait till the old woman became well so that we could play with our ball again. But she never got better. The days came and went. We just roamed in the lanes, among the wheat fields, and on the threshing floor, not doing much.

*

Autumn arrived. The harvest was over and the peasants began storing the meagre wheat grains they had produced in small drums in their hovels. The women became busy, hanging bunches of grapes on strings stretched across the rafters in rooms, spreading them on the roofs to make raisins, or boiling them in large cauldrons to make *shireh* to be eaten during the cold season.

The village school opened. We sat on shaky wooden benches in the classroom and furiously copied whatever the teacher chalked on the blackboard. Whenever the teacher was facing the blackboard or dozing off in his chair, I lifted my head from my notebook and gazed out of the window into the deserted school grounds, hoping for playtime to start so that we could go out and play with the only ball shared by all the boys.

After leaving school in the afternoons, our dog-eared notebooks tucked under our arms, we wandered in the dusty lanes, sat beside the springs, and threw stones at sparrows that splashed about on the edge of the water. Around late afternoon, swarms of rooks appeared from nowhere, flew everywhere, and perched on the edges of the ruined walls of the old fortresses of feudal lords, dead and gone long ago. The rooks cawed and cawed, stretching their necks towards the purple-hued mountains that bounded the horizon. With their din, the milky-blue dusk peered from behind the mountains and began to creep over the village.

*

Winter was upon us. The mud-brick houses became buried under a thick carpet of snow. The village folk crept into their hovels and sat around their *korsis*, munching raisins, drinking tea, smoking opium, sucking at their *chibouks*, and gossiping endlessly about their relatives and neighbours. We spent oppressive hours in the school. Every day dusk arrived too soon. When we left the school, the snow on the bare trees glistened in the milky-blue half-dark. The snow was so high we nearly sank in it. The noises of the village sounded as if they were coming from creatures buried under heaps of snow.

As we knew that the friend of the worn-out peasant was a scythe-maker, we imagined that he had almost certainly torn our ball into pieces to put its rubber to different uses.

*

Around springtime the snow began to melt, making the lanes and pathways muddy. The village was filled once again with cheerful hustle and bustle. The peasants were out and about, preparing for the *Nowruz* Festival. People had put aside their usual squabbles and were kind to each other. Tiny buds began to swell on the branches of the trees.

Whenever my friends and I passed in front of the worn-out peasant's hovel, I poked my head into it. Every time I saw fewer and fewer hens clucking around the sickly cockerel.

One day, after the *Nowruz* holiday, as my friend and I were passing in front of the hovel, I peeped inside and saw only one hen was sitting on the filthy ground, clucking quietly. The sickly cockerel was doing its best to mount her, but kept slipping every time down her featherless back.

"You know what, Ahmad," I said in a low voice.

"What?"

"There's only one hen left."

"Didn't you know that?" Ahmad exclaimed, "People have seen Safarali Cholagh slitting the throats of his hens at the edge of the brook. I think he's slaughtered all of them except this one?"

"Do you reckon he's going to kill this one, too?" I asked, looking inside the hovel.

"Course not," replied Ahmad, looking at me as a wise man regards an imbecile.

"Why not?"

"Bah, honestly, Amir," he said. "I thought you knew better. He keeps the frigging hen alive so that it can copulate with the cockerel in order to lay eggs. I suppose he boils the eggs to feed his sick mother."

"This hen is the lucky one, then," I said, smiling.

"Definitely." Ahmad chuckled. "Having had a lucky escape so far, I don't think she and the cockerel have long to enjoy one another's company. The way they're overdoing it, they'll exhaust one another and will soon end up in the cooking pot!"

Whenever we sat in the mosque, listening to the village mollah, we prayed to God so that the mother of the worn-out peasant soon got well again so that we could go on playing with our ball, if it was still there, that was.

*

Summer arrived. One cool morning around mid-June, we lined up as usual in the dusty school grounds and sang the national anthem, praying to God to keep the Shah and the Queen alive and healthy to look after us. When the head-teacher finished his customary speech about the importance of being literate and remaining loyal to the Shah and the country, he informed us that that day was the last day of the school. He warned us to be good during the summer break, as he would sometimes see our parents in the mosque, the main thoroughfare, and the fields and would ask them about us.

"So be good and help your parents during your long break," he concluded.

The last day of school being the best day of the school year for us, we just sat in the shade of the wall and chattered endlessly about the carefree summer days ahead, during which we would be as free as the birds of the air. When in the classroom, all I did was sit on the bench and daydream.

Around four in the afternoon we all dashed out of the school, all running in different directions, like calves let out of the barn for the first time. Once a safe distance from the school, we tore our notebooks into shreds, chucked them on the ground, trampled on them like monkeys gone berserk, smashed our inkpots into the mud-brick walls, and frolicked around like lunatics let out of the asylum.

Unburdened from everything to do with schooling, from that day on we set upon our own ways of educating ourselves. We roamed in the village lanes and alleyways, among the golden wheat fields that roasted in the sun, in the ancient ruins, near the spring source and on the threshing floors. We shot countless number of sparrows with our catapults, teased the young girls carrying pitchers of water on their shoulders, sat in the shade of trees and daydreamed till we felt dozy.

Summer days came and passed without us having our ball back to play with.

*

As the summer holiday drew to the end we became sadder and sadder. We did our best to enjoy whatever we did, but at the back of our minds was the thought of tedious school hours with endless dictations, arithmetic, and the history of kings and their never-ending battles with other kings to grab more lands.

The day before the school was supposed to open, Ahmad and I happened to pass through the lane in which the worn-out peasant lived. From a distance I saw him perched on top of a rickety ladder, hammering a black piece of cloth on top of the door of his hovel. A small group of women, all wrapped up in black chadors, had gathered outside the door. The women, one at a time, stepped inside the hovel. No sooner they were inside than they began to shriek and wail.

"Ahmad," I said under my breath, nudging him.

"What?

"Do you think the old woman is dead?"

"It looks like it," said he. "Maybe God listened to us by taking away Safarali's mother so that we could once again play with our ball."

"If it's still there, that is," I said.

A few other peasants soon emerged from an alleyway at the end of the lane and walked towards the hovel. By this time the worn-out peasant had come down the ladder and was looking up at the black rag. The peasants greeted him, all weeping loudly. They then lugged the ladder inside the hovel.

Having nothing to do, we stood in the shade of the wall, waiting to see what happened next. It was not long before the same peasants walked out of the hovel, bearing the ladder on their shoulders. On top of the ladder was a corpse, wrapped in a dusty, tattered kilim. The women followed the ladder, wailing and beating themselves, scattering dust and with bits of dung clinging to their chadors. The small procession moved in the direction of the mosque at the foot of the graveyard.

Once again silence returned to the lane.

"Ahmad," I said quietly.

"Hmm?"

"There's no one in the hovel now."

"So?"

"Let's take a look at it."

"Why?"

"We might find our ball there."

"I'm scared."

"Scared of what?"

"Someone has just died there."

"But they took her away."

I managed to persuade Ahmad. We stood beside the door that was open a crack, like the mouth of a dead man. I peeked inside. My eyes fell upon the scythe-maker, who was sitting on his haunches leaning against the wall, sharpening his scythe. Beside him on the floor was a large round bundle. After a while he extracted his handkerchief from his waistcoat pocket and wiped his eyes. He then began to untie the knot of the bundle. As he did so, I followed the movement of his calloused fingers as they worked at the tight knot.

"You know what, Ahmad?" I whispered.

"What?"

"I think we'll have our ball soon," I said and asked Ahmad to take a peek inside.

"The scythe-maker's untying his bundle, that's all," said Ahmad, turning towards me.

"I know," said I. "Our ball could be in that bundle."

"How do you know?"

"Because it's so round."

I peeped inside again. Once the cloth was spread wide open on the floor, I saw in the middle of it nothing but chunks of stale bread.

The following day after school, as we were passing through the same lane, we stopped and gazed up at the black rag for a while as it flapped in the warm afternoon breeze. All of a sudden the skinny cockerel hopped out of the hovel and began strutting around, pecking at the dung pieces. Red patches of skin shone from among its ashen feathers. We waited a while. I peeked inside the hovel. The lucky hen was nowhere to be heard or seen.

Romance in the Lane

The bulk of Agha Kamal's body resembled one of those long, oval Persian melons, crowned by his small head, on top of which was a bald patch, bordered with thinning frizzy hair. His matchstick arms tapered towards his skinny hands and his spindly legs hung from the bottom of his torso. His tiny feet stuck out from the bottom of his short crinkled trousers like a pair of dormice.

His wife, Zeenat Khanum, known in the lane as Zeenat *Kalaantar* for taking upon herself the role of local sheriff, was a buxom woman with a round face and a complexion as ruddy as that of an overripe pomegranate. Her hands were the size and colour of a pair of lamb shoulders. She had a booming voice to put one in mind of the horn blown at doomsday to wake the dead for the final judgement.

Every late afternoon, during hot summer days, her *chador* wrapped around her waist and knotted in front, she would stomp out of her house clutching the end of a black hosepipe to sprinkle the dusty patch in front of the door. As she did so, the hosepipe curled and wriggled, serpent-like, behind her, adding a greater air of menace to her presence.

Upon seeing her, all the urchins in the lane, running after a deflated plastic ball, would freeze like chicks seeing the shadow of a great eagle hovering overhead. As she carried on with her sprinkling, she would glare from time to time at each one of us, making us nearly wet our pants.

Agha Kamal was a fabrics pedlar, wandering in the lanes in the neighbourhood, going from door to door, selling his fabrics to women who stood in their doorways touching and feeling his cloths, haggling and flirting with him at the same time. It was common knowledge in the lane that he was completely under his wife's thumb. Every evening around supper time, as we stayed up till very late in the lane, playing our games, we would hear Zeenat Kalaantar shrieking in her yard, followed soon by Agha Kamal being shoved through the door while she stood behind him in the doorway under the arch gripping a broom like a cave-dweller guarding her cave.

"What sin have I committed to deserve such a good-for-nothing husband?" she would bellow, brandishing the broom and sending shivers down our spines. "Oh, why in God's name did my parents marry me off to him!"

We would stop whatever we were doing in the half-dark to gaze at the unhappy Agha Kamal, who would sink down on his knees, huddling by the shut door. He would clutch his head, caressing his bald patch and running his fingers through the wisp of hair at the back of his head. Leaving him brooding over his sorrows, we would go back to our games in the dim light of the only street lamp in the middle of the lane.

Half an hour would not be out than the door of the house would be flung open and Zeenat Kalaantar would emerge, still gripping the ominous broom.

"Come on, Kamal, get up and come in," she would say in a sugary voice, prodding him with the broom. "Don't you want to have some tea?"

Agha Kamal would get up and slip back through the door, as docile as a lamb.

*

I reckon the best day up till then in Agha Kamal's life was the day when my father had a row over him with Zeenat Kalaantar.

That day we were playing our noisy football in the lane. One of the boys kicked the ball so high that it landed on the low roof of Agha Kamal's house. As always, I stood against the wall of the house with my hands clasped in front of me to hoist a smaller boy up to the roof to fetch the ball. After throwing the ball down he dangled from the edge of the roof, trying to put his feet on my shoulders. It was exactly at that moment that I heard Zeenat Kalaantar's thunderous roar echoing in her yard. Scared out of my wits, I became glued to the wall. Paralyzed by fear, the boy began to jiggle nervously above me like a freaked-out lizard. It would be very cowardly of me to leave him in that state, run off and hide in the narrow alley at the end of the lane, so, on second thoughts, I summoned up whatever courage was left to me and stayed put to help him climb down.

It was, alas, too late, because at that instant Zeenat Kalaantar crashed into the lane, fuming like an enraged bull. Upon spotting us, she grasped my head in her powerful hands, pulled me off the wall, and lifted me up like a sack of potatoes, screeching at close range to my face all sorts of swearwords in the order of: you misbegotten jinni, you spoilt little brat, you son of the devil! My little friend, who had taken fright at seeing such a monstrous apparition, remained dangling, motionless.

That was when my father walked into the lane in his full policeman regalia.

Upon seeing my father, she let me drop, and directed all the swearwords she had in her stock of foul language to him.

"What sort of policeman are you, who cannot even discipline his own little monsters?" Zeenat Kalaantar concluded her outburst, reminding my father of his law-enforcing duties.

"Consider yourself very lucky that I'm not answering you back, you foul-mouthed, cantankerous woman." My father addressed her calmly and politely as policemen do, after listening to her patiently. "I only keep quiet out of respect for Agha Kamal."

This comment cut Zeenat Kalaantar to the quick. Salamander-like, her cheeks turned into the colour of a rotten pomegranate, making her look even more hideous. She surely would not bleed if you stuck a knife into her cheeks.

"*Bah, bah*, since when has Agha Kamal joined the ranks of respectable human beings?" she rumbled at my father. "Pity you're a policeman, otherwise I would teach you a lesson or two as well."

Agha Kamal, crushed, just squatted against the wall of the house, abjectly eyeing my father from time to time.

"Go on, say something, you wimpy bumpkin," Zeenat Kalaantar shrieked at her husband, slapping his head hard, "instead of cowering there like a wretched mouse."

Ignoring her, Agha Kamal got up and ambled inside the house. Zeenat Kalaantar, her arms akimbo, glared around at the idle onlookers, who by now had made a ring round her. Seeing her blood-shot eyes, they backed away mutely, as if from a mad dog. She then turned round, strode to the door, slamming it behind her. Her loud growling could be heard echoing in the short passageway. An ominous silence soon fell upon the house.

"Go back to your homes now." My father walked up to the spectators. "The *ta'zieh* is over." He helped the dangling boy down, tapping his head kindly, and said, "Run off to your home." Upon which the boy sprang to his feet and scuttled back to his house, pulling up his trousers to cover his dusty bottom. I was surprised at seeing my father so cool after being assailed by all those colourful swearwords.

"I put her in her place, the shameless woman!" my father muttered, gripping my hand. "Let's go home, it's supper time."

By restoring Agha Kamal's dignity in the eyes of the neighbours, my father had ridiculed Zeenat Kalaantar. Whether he did this on purpose or not, I could never tell, as my father never got into arguments with the neighbours over our games. He was an even-tempered man, my father was. God bless his soul.

This action on the part of my father, however, made matters much worse. Not having anybody to bully, Zeenat Kalaantar vented her rage on her wretched husband by kicking him out of the house on a regular basis, even when it was pouring with rain. On rainy days Agha Kamal, a plastic bag pulled over his head, would squat against the wall of his house like a mongrel dog. To keep him company, we would sometimes sit beside him, chatting among ourselves as if he was not there. He would listen without uttering a word. As we had piles of homework to do, we would, one by one, slip away, leaving him alone in the rain.

After supper, to see if he was still there, I would sneak out on the excuse of going to the junk-room at the far end of the courtyard to put bits of mulberry leaves in the matchbox in which I kept my silkworms. Once in the room, I would climb on the large chest, draw the curtain aside a little and peep out of the casement. To my surprise, Agha Kamal still used to sit quietly under the rain like a soaked rat. After an hour, Zeenat Kalaantar would silently pull the door open a crack, peer into the lane, and vanish into the passageway, leaving the door open. Evidently, the open door acted like a signal to Agha Kamal, signifying that he should get back into the house. Happy to see that the wretched man had gone back inside, I would then return to my silkworms that were munching away at the fresh mulberry leaves.

*

On one of those rainy evenings, as I was spying on Agha Kamal from my secret observation post, a figure, wrapped up in black chador, appeared from the end of the lane, walking towards him. She was carrying a tin tray on which was placed a glass of tea in a saucer beside which were a few small sugar lumps. She stood beside Agha Kamal and placed the tray in front of him. When she turned to look around I recognised Shahla Khanum, known in the lane as Shahla Namaki for being a seductress. As Agha Kamal popped the sugar cubes into his mouth and gulped down the tea, he kept looking up at her, his expression one of mingled gratitude and admiration.

As the lane was a cul-de-sac, everyone knew everyone else's secrets: whose wife was cheating on her husband, whose husband was after another man's wife, which lonely young woman was on the game, who worked as a part-time pimp to make ends meet, who collaborated with the Shah's secret police grassing on the young student lodgers, who were the child molesters. Everybody knew that Shahla Namaki's husband had run off, two years earlier, with the wife of Mehdi Bighavareh and no one had ever heard of them since. Shahla Namaki now lived with her ailing mother, always on the lookout for the men in the lane who were trapped in unhappy marriages.

Agha Kamal and Shahla Namaki went on talking quietly to one another. Whatever secrets they were exchanging with each other made Agha Kamal smile, every so often looking up at Shahla Namaki as an imbecile looks at a beautiful woman. I had never seen him smile like that.

This secret love affair carried on for a while. By an unwritten agreement with Shahla Namaki, whenever Agha Kamal pushed the tray of tea behind him, I would know that Zeenat Kalaantar had left the door open, letting him know he should at once go back into the house. Upon seeing this signal, Shahla Namaki would pick up the tea tray and scurry back to her home. Agha Kamal would then stand up and saunter back into his house, casting sidelong glances back at Shahla Namaki. Once under the arch, he would throw her a final amorous peek, as a billy goat does to a nanny goat, smiling in complicity.

I became the unseen witness to this romantic backstairs tryst. By and by Shahla Namaki's beauty did the trick. Agha Kamal became so infatuated with the lonely woman that he threw all caution to the winds. Not a wise thing to do, I felt, knowing his troubles as I did! He became so wrapped up in the pleasure of Shahla's company that, most of the time, he forgot about the tea-tray-hiding ploy. Knowing what kind of woman Zeenat was, Shahla sometimes had to plead with Agha Kamal to get up and go in before his wife found out something fishy was going on. On the occasions when the door of the house remained open, gaping like the mouth of a dead man, I became more and more anxious that any minute Zeenat Kalaantar might storm out of the house, and only the devil knew what she would do! Sometimes, as I looked at the open door, I would be tempted to open the casement, shout and warn the lovers about the imminent danger lurking in the shadowy courtyard behind the door. But on second thoughts, being a morbidly curious boy, I thought I'd rather wait to see what action would come out of that tragi-comedy going on before my eyes. Anyway, who was I to meddle with the affairs of the grown-ups? At the time I was a mere boy.

*

Agha Kamal's carelessness in not standing up on time and walking into his house raised Zeenat Kalaantar's suspicions. One evening, as I was spying as usual on the secret lovers wrapped up in their intimate talk, I heard a thunderous roar. Who else could it be but Zeenat

Kalaantar? She stormed out of the house, wrapping her chador round her waist, knotting it over her front. Upon seeing her, Shahla Namaki took fright, picked up the tea-tray, and scampered towards the end of the lane. Zeenat Kalaantar chased her like a maddened rhinoceros. Hearing her shriek, the neighbours opened their casements and stuck their heads out, leaning their elbows on the sills, to see who was having a brawl with whom this time. In order not to miss the show, I dashed out of the room and into the lane. A handful of neighbours were already out standing in their doorways watching the two women, chuckling and cracking jokes.

I joined the other urchins who had made a ring round the pair, grinning broadly. Zeenat Kalaantar had fallen on Shahla Namaki like a bird of prey, raining slaps and kicks all over her body, still wrapped in her chador. In the twilight zone of the lane, Shahla Namaki's naked body gleamed every so often like white marble from under her dusty chador. Her clothes were torn into tatters.

"You husband-thief!" Zeenat Kalaantar squawked, huffing and puffing like a witch in the half-darkness. "You're now offering my good man tea to lure him to your filthy bed. All the neighbours know why your husband ran off with Esmat Khaldar, because you couldn't have enough of every pedlar and hawker who passed your door."

"I swear to Imam Reza I've not done anything wrong, Zeenat Khanum," Shahla Namaki whimpered, cowering under Zeenat's blows, while trying desperately to cover herself at the same time. "I just felt sorry for your husband sitting out there like an orphan and thought I'd give him a glass of tea to cheer him up a bit."

"...so that you can cheer him up a bit later the way you cheered up the other men, hey!" Zeenat Kalaantar croaked like an old crow, tugging at Shahla's tangled hair from which hung gobbets of spittle. "I know too well what lies behind your charity tea, you man-hunter."

The more Shahla Namaki pleaded, the more enraged Zeenat Kalaantar became. Seeing his secret admirer being battered mercilessly by his wife, Agha Kamal summoned up his courage and ran to her rescue. Alas, he was no match for that amazon of a wife! One well-aimed back-kick delivered to his belly by Zeenat Kalaantar was sufficient to send him reeling backwards like a melon fallen from the packsaddle of a donkey into the gutter in the middle of the lane.

Moved by pity for Shahla Namaki, two of the more god-fearing, kindly-disposed women ran out of their houses and hurled themselves into the fray, trying to free the bruised and battered victim from the clutches of that warrior woman.

"For Hazrat Abbas's sake, Zeenat Khanum," one of the women screamed, putting herself in serious peril by trying to push her away, "show some mercy to this wretched woman and let her go!"

"Yes, let her go, Zeenat Khanum," chipped in the second woman. "You've taught her a good lesson. She'll never come near your husband again."

Out of some respect for the two women, Zeenat Kalaantar left Shahla Namaki in the middle of the lane, half covered by her ripped clothes, huddling into herself and weeping quietly. One of the women took her chador off and threw it over Shahla's body.

Fuming, Zeenat Kalaantar turned back, stomping towards her husband who lay sprawled in the gutter, helplessly watching the scene. She stood beside her guilty-looking man, arms pressed on her hips, glowering down at him.

"Come on, get out of my sight before I thrash you into a pulp, you crafty fox," she croaked, taking off one of her slippers and slapping his head and face with it. "If I ever see you so much as glancing at that woman again I'll tear both of you into shreds!"

Just then I saw my father, in his pyjamas and gripping his opium pipe, emerge from the house. He strode up to Zeenat Kalaantar.

"That's enough, woman," he announced like a man who had smoked a half-a-roll of opium. "You've no kernel of shame left in you. You've humiliated these two wretches and caused mayhem at this late hour of the night, bringing out these hard-working folk from their homes." He then added after a pause, "My patience is running out. If you carry on like this, I'll know how to deal with you. Now take this poor man and get into your house."

Then the unthinkable happened. Zeenat Kalaantar, all of a sudden, burst into tears and began to weep, howling like a gypsy. A profound hush fell on the bystanders. They backed off, returning to their homes one by one, glancing over their shoulders in disbelief. Zeenat Kalaantar rushed into her yard, followed by her husband.

*

A week was not out before Shahla Namaki left our lane, never to appear in the neighbourhood again. Peace and quiet returned to the lane and the folk went about their humdrum lives.

A week after Shahla Namaki's disappearance, one late afternoon, as I was playing knucklebones with my friends at the foot of the lamppost, a clutch of women gathered beside the doorway of Vaji Khanum's house to gossip about the latest scandals in the lane. As I heard them mention Shahla Namaki's name, I pricked up my ears and managed to catch some of their talk, pretending all the while I was absorbed in our game.

"The way Shahla was carrying on, she'll definitely end up in *Shahr-e No*," Akram Khanum said.

"I don't think so, love," Zari Khanum pointed out. "Being attractive, she is more likely to work as a showgirl in one of those cabarets in Lalezar."

"I reckon you're right, Zari." Eshrat Khanum spoke from under her chador. "Do you remember her belly-dancing for a roomful of women at the night of Hajji Toopchi's daughter's wedding?"

"How can we forget," Zari Khanum and Akram Khanum chorused, "especially as she did it as naked as the day she was born!"

"But she only did that for us women, sweetheart," Shamsi Khanum joined in.

"If she could do it for us, Shamsi *joon*," said Eshrat Khanum, "she can easily do it for a roomful of drunken men if she becomes a kept woman for one of those dumb buggers in the fedora in downtown Tehran."

I tossed the knucklebones on the dusty ground, slapping my knee. I then nudged my brother.

"Did you hear that, Nasser?" I said under my breath.

"Hear what?" Nasser said, gathering the knucklebones and shaking them in his cupped hands.

"They're talking about Shahla Namaki's belly-dancing at the wedding night of Hajji Toopchi's daughter when you and I hid under a table and watched her naked body," I said.

"Oh, yes," said Nasser, grinning from ear to ear. "What a white body she had! Pity the women found out about us and pushed us out of the room."

Agha Kamal had never again sat outside his house till that fateful evening.

As we were noisily kicking the football around, I saw Agha Kamal come out of his house and sit against the wall. A moment later Zeenat Kalaantar emerged quietly out of the yard and stood beside her husband, pleading to him in a low voice to get back into the house. Ignoring her, Agha Kamal kept glancing in the direction of the street at the other end of the lane. Zeenat Kalaantar did her best as a good wife would do to coax her husband to come in. All her efforts fell on deaf ears. Agha Kamal just sat there like a sulking brat, staring into the void at the end of the lane. Downcast, Zeenat Kalaantar returned to the yard, leaving the door open.

We went on playing till late. Every now and then I looked to see if Agha Kamal was still there. He surely was, hunched up, glancing every so often in the direction of the street. A few neighbours carrying *sangak* bread, fruit and vegetables in paper packets scurried phantom-like along the walls, silently slipping into their houses and shutting the doors behind them. Some parents appeared at their doorways, calling out to my friends to get in as it was supper time. I was left outside with my brother and two other boys. As we stood under the lamppost, debating what games to play or where to roam about the next day, I saw Agha Kamal stand up and saunter towards the street. Once at the angle of the vacant lot and the street, he looked around as if waiting for someone. He then walked back into the lane, sat near his doorway, as a thief does in the half-dark, biding his time. He did not, however, go into his house.

My brother and I said goodnight to our friends and walked towards our house. Before shutting the door behind me I cast a last glance into the lane. I saw Agha Kamal scuttling along the gutter towards the street. As I peered into the gloom, I could just make out a figure in a black veil standing outside the grocer's. Agha Kamal stood beside the figure, then they both crossed the street and vanished into the shadows of the dimly-lit lane opposite.

*

We never saw Agha Kamal again. This event set the tongues of the chadored scandalmongers in the lane wagging, spreading the wildest notions about his sudden disappearance. I heard about all these speculations while I stood in the queues to buy bread from the baker's, butter and cheese from the dairy shop, or fruit from the grocer's, or simply playing with other guttersnipes in the lane.

"Agha Kamal has no doubt returned to his native village having had enough of his dragon of a wife," one woman would say to another while waiting for the cucumber pedlar to weigh up the cucumbers on his dented scales.

"The poor man had suffered so much in the hands of that ill-tempered woman he made up his mind to run away," another neighbour would air her views to her friend while haggling with the grapes vendor.

My father, however, being a policeman, had a different, more realistic opinion about the matter.

"I'm sure Agha Kamal had arranged a secret rendezvous with Shahla Namaki somewhere, either in Tehran or some other city," he said one afternoon to my uncle, who sat before the brazier inhaling a good puff of opium smoke. "We deal with a lot of cases like these every day: young folk who escape from their native villages to come to this whorehouse of Tehran to seek non-existent fortunes, young women who leave their fanatical fathers and brothers, young men who elope with the wives of others."

After a while the neighbours forgot all about Shahla Namaki and Agha Kamal as new and more exciting scandals cropped up in other households to keep their fertile imaginations going. Untroubled by what was going on in the world of the grown-ups, we went on playing every day in the lane till late.

Every afternoon Zeenat Kalaantar would silently slip out of her house, hose down the small patch in front of the doorway and sit down, leaning against the wall. When we became tired of playing we would sit against the opposite wall, chatting about our kites, our silkworms, and which pretty girl in the lane fancied which one of us. Sometimes I would cast a furtive glance at Zeenat Kalaantar as she sat huddled up against the wall, her eyes fixed in the direction of the street. The neighbours passed her by without even looking at her. After an hour or so of staring at the street, she would wipe her tears, stand up with difficulty and walk back into her house, noiselessly shutting the door behind her.

Batool

I was a boy of around nine years old when Batool appeared in our household.

That summer morning I was sitting in the empty room at the far end of our courtyard, putting the final touches to my kite, when my mother walked into the yard with Batool. It was the holy month of Moharram and my mother had met her the day before in the *tekieh* held in the yard of one of our neighbours. They had soon struck up a friendship.

As time passed my mother grew fond of Batool, inviting her to come to our house whenever she left the orphanage in which she had grown up. Batool occasionally went out to buy bits and pieces from haberdashers' shops to make handicrafts such as gloves, bead purses, and scarves. She earned a meagre living by selling them to crafts shops. I reckon at the time she was about sixteen years old. She was sweet and affectionate with a broad smile. Quite short, she had a round face, hazel brown eyes and sensual lips. She was always dressed in a short skirt showing her shapely ivory-coloured legs. She spoke with a lisp and laughed heartily at the slightest thing she found amusing. When she left the orphanage, she would come straight to our house. I knew she came only to see my mother, whom she loved so much.

Throughout the long summer holidays I would sit, some mornings, in the shade of the small oleander tree beside the flower bed in our courtyard, making my kites. Around midmorning my mother and Batool would come and squat near the *hauz*, nattering about neighbourhood gossip and what went on in the orphanage, while dipping the clothes in the water and wringing them. At moments like that, one would imagine they were mother and daughter.

One day around noon, as I was sitting on the step of the passage leading to the kitchen reading a children's magazine, I heard Batool talk about her mother and father for the first time. As she recounted her story, the shadow of a rueful smile flitted across her lips:

"I wath a little girl the day my mother wath killed by my father. Ath I wath thitting on the edge of the gutter in the lane playing with other girlth, I heard a shriek coming from inthide of the lodging houthe in which we lived. Our next door neighbour rushed out of her houthe and ran inthide. Then other neighbourth gathered around the door. I that there, frightened out of my witth. I thaw two of the lodgerth run out of the houthe calling for thomeone to go and find a politheman. One of the neighbourth came to me and lifted me up, kithing and hugging me. I had a vague idea that thomething wath not right. Thoon two polithemen arrived and took my father away. No one told me what had happened to my mum for fear of making me upthet."

"So where did they take you?" my mother asked as she dipped a shirt in the water.

"Ath I had no relativeth in Tehran they took me to thith orphanage," Batool lisped, wringing a pair of trousers to squeeze out the water.

"Did you find out what had happened that day?"

"Much later on when I wath a bit older, one of the neighbourth, who hath remained a friend to me to thith day, told me the whole thtory. My father, while breaking the large sugar cone into thmall pietheth with an adthe, had, in a fit of rage, smashed my mother'th thkull. They locked him up for life," Batool explained. After a short silence she said

"Later on I heard from people that the judge, reading the verdict to my father, had told him that the adthe ith commonly uthed by men to break large sugar coneth into thmaller lumpth, not to crack open people'th skullth. Luckily, the judge, being in a good humour and unusually lenient on the day of the final verdict, did not condemn my father to be hanged in a public thquare, thententhing him inthtead to life imprithonment."

*

Having heard this tragic story, my mother became increasingly attached to Batool. She, in turn, liked my mother because she did not feel sorry for her as did other women in our lane. My mother treated her as an equal and quite normal. Batool saw, no doubt, in my mother a substitute for her lost one.

"There's nothing wrong with having grown up in an orphanage," my mother would say to our neighbours when they dropped in to borrow a cauldron, large pots and pans, or just to have a chat. "Batool is so kind and lovely. I can have a bit of a gossip and a good laugh with her."

Batool came to our house every Thursday and stayed over until Friday afternoon, when she had to return to the orphanage. By and by, she became almost a member of our family.

Her regular weekly visits to our home attracted my young uncles and the young men among our relatives into the house, frequenting us even more often than before, like flies that appear from nowhere to buzz around sweetmeats. They found all sorts of flimsy excuses such as helping my dad or carrying the fruit and vegetables from the marketplace to come into our house just to talk to and flirt with Batool. They soon began to compete with each other, asking her out to go with them to the cinema at the roundabout at the end of our street or to ice-cream parlours. Upon hearing them, she just blushed furiously, her cheeks becoming as crimson as rose-petals in spring, and laughed her delightful, silvery laughter, politely turning down their gallant invitations.

Realising that Batool was one of those girls who had chosen to remain an eternal sister to men, they soon abandoned all hope of courting her as a possible future bride. Their visits became less frequent, leaving Batool in peace.

"Maybe this is one of her misfortunes, too," my mother would sigh to my father, handing him a glass of tea after his afternoon nap.

When Batool stayed with us she did all our household chores. It was as if she desperately wanted to belong somewhere—to a home, a family. With her kindness, she won my brother and me over, making us abandon the mischievous pranks we had sometimes played on her.

When in our house, she washed the tea glasses, filled up the samovar, prepared the tea, kept an eye on the pots on the stove in our small kitchen at the back of the house, rinsed and chopped the vegetables in the tiny inner courtyard beside the kitchen, and washed the clothes in the *hauz*. She did her best to make everyone happy.

As the time passed, we grew so accustomed to her coming to our house every Thursday that if one day she was late we would become very worried, counting the minutes to hearing the familiar knock on the door.

Batool gained a unique place in my mother's heart, even though she had three daughters of her own. Soon the other young girls among our relatives visited our house less and less and stopped coming altogether. I suppose they felt jealous of Batool, who had become so dear to us all.

Batool's relationship with my family had become firmly established—until one Thursday, towards the end of the summer holidays, she did not show up. We waited another week. Again, she did not turn up. Two weeks went by and still there was no sign or news of Batool.

Anxious to know what had happened to her, my mother and I took a bus to the orphanage in downtown Tehran to find out what had happened to her. We were told that Batool had gone home with her father.

"But we thought her father was in prison for the rest of his life," my mother said to the woman in charge of the orphanage.

"Not any more," the woman replied. "He and some others were pardoned by the Shah on the commemoration of his coming to the throne."

"Do you know where they live?" my mother asked. "Do you think you can give us the address, khanum?"

"Are you relatives of hers?"

"Not really," said my mother. "But she's almost like a daughter to me. She comes every Thursday to spend the weekend with us."

"What's your name, khanum?"

"Mohtaram."

"Batool talked a lot about you," said the woman, smiling for the first time. "She liked you a lot."

She wrote the address on a piece of paper and handed it over to my mother.

*

The following day, around mid-morning, my mother put on her chador, wrapped some *sangak* bread and cheese in a cloth, and we got on a bus to go and find Batool. She and her father lived near the Shah Abdolazim shrine, down in the south of Tehran.

After a one-hour drive, we got out of the bus and wandered through winding lanes and narrow alleys in the middle of which ran slime-choked gutters. Swarms of ragamuffins played in the dust and scampered along the gutters. Finally we found the house, tucked away under a crumbling brick arch at the end of a narrow alley. My mother grabbed the rusty doorknocker and banged it on the door a few times. An ill-tempered woman, veiled in a black chador, opened the door a chink.

"Who do you want?" she asked, eyeing my mother and me with the suspicious air of the downtown dwellers.

"Do Batool and her father live here?" my mother asked.

"Yes," the woman muttered.

"Can we see her, please?" my mother asked politely.

"Whom shall I say it is?"

"Tell her Mohtaram Khanum has come to see her."

The woman slammed the door in our faces, making the doorknocker rattle.

"Ohoy, Batool!" I heard her shriek, echoing in the yard behind the door. "A woman called Mohtaram wants to see you."

I heard the sound of hurried footsteps coming towards the door. After a few seconds the door was opened and Batool appeared in the doorway. She looked drawn and pale, with sunken eyes, but still managed a cheerful laugh, albeit a forced one.

"Mohtaram Khanum," she joyfully exclaimed, throwing herself round my mother's neck. "Oh, my God, it'th you!"

Upon spotting me behind my mother, she ruffled my hair in her kindly manner.

"I'll come and vithit you thoon, Mohtaram Khanum, promithe," she said, struggling to hold back the tears welling in her eyes.

She did not invite us in. I reckoned she was ashamed of something, something she did not want us to see.

"Don't forget to come and see us some time," my mother, who understood everything, reminded her, giving her an affectionate hug. We then said goodbye and left Batool, who stood in the doorway watching us go.

My mother and I walked out of the lane in silence. Every so often, I cast surreptitious glances up at her profile. Sunk in deep thought, she looked like a mother whose newly-married daughter has just left the family home for good.

"Let's go to the Ebn-e Ba'ab-e-vey cemetery to sit and have a morsel," she said all of a sudden, grabbing my hand with her strong one, made rough with years of washing and scrubbing.

This was a welcome suggestion as I was getting hungry.

Once in the cemetery, she found a gravestone just near the main gate that had been recently sprinkled with water by a grave-washer. My mother untied the cheese-and-bread cloth and spread it over the gravestone beside which we sat and began to tuck in.

It was now afternoon. The air smelt of autumn already. The graves shimmered in the haze of the afternoon sun. I looked around as I munched my bread and cheese. Black-chadored women shambled on the dusty paths between graves, their chadors like the wings of ravens fluttering in the fresh autumnal breeze, and offered votive dates to other visitors. The lamentations of these women mingled with the non-stop droning of swarms of mollahs and professional prayer-readers, scuttling like black cockroaches among the graves, praying in Arabic for the souls of the departed. The raucous cawing of flocks of crows wheeling in the clear sky filled the air, joining the mayhem and adding to the melancholy air of the cemetery. A few of them swooped down to land on the graves, raising clouds of dust and hopping around for scraps of food left by the mourners. The silence of the cemetery was shattered every now and then by black-clad, stubbly men who carried on their shoulders a corpse stretched on a ladder like a gigantic carrot carefully swathed in a dusty, ragged kilim. They wept and slapped their foreheads, chanting prayers in Arabic that I did not understand.

My mother and I went on watching the noisy, motley processions entering the cemetery every ten minutes.

"Don't know what to say," my mother sighed, waving her arm in defeat, like a woman who does not understand the tricks blind fate plays on us wretched humans. "Poor girl. Thank God she's now *somehow* settled and doesn't live in that orphanage."

As she gazed vacantly at a small huddle of women sitting around a fresh mound of earth, weeping and cackling quietly like jackdaws, I saw her eyes fill with tears. She kept wiping them with the hem of her chador.

Throughout the journey home on the bus she remained quiet, gazing out of the window.

*

Batool, however, did not keep to her promise and never showed up again in our household. Some Friday mornings, as I sat in the backroom doing my homework, I heard my mother talking about Batool to one of our neighbours in the quiet backyard. On hearing Batool's name, I would peep out from behind the curtain. My mother, as she chatted away, looked as if she did not know what to make of Batool's not keeping her promise. Tears glistened in her eyes, followed by the merest shadow of a smile flickering on her lips.

Days flashed by and months and years passed. Batool faded in our memories, her face and laughter swallowed up by the past, leaving nothing but occasional scraps of recollection.

One day, many years later, when we were all travelling back in a coach from the holy city of Mashhad, there was an accident. My mother and brother died instantly, but the rest of us survived. My father never recovered from his loss. My sisters and I did our best to console him and help him to cope, but soon after this incident two of my elder sisters got married and left home, leaving the youngest one to look after my father.

At the time I had taken charge of my father's job in the bazaar, as his ailments prevented him from working in the shop for long hours. Every noontime I would go home with packets of fruit in my hand to have lunch with my father, keeping him company. Every Friday morning all three of us made a bundle of bread, cheese, and dates and went to the Ebn-e Bab-e-vey cemetery to sit near the graves of my mother and brother to remember them by reciting a few prayers, and to have our own sort of picnic there.

*

One fine day in spring, a few days before *Nowruz*, I returned home around noon to find everything spick and span. The house looked as if someone had been doing spring-cleaning the whole morning. The *korsi* was put away, all the carpets were swept, the windows polished, the yard was hosed down, and the flowers in the flower-beds had been watered. The air in the house smelt fresh and the smell of my favourite food wafted out from the kitchen.

I walked gingerly across the yard and entered into the half-dark, cool kitchen. I saw a middle-aged woman with a slightly hunched shoulder, wearing a flowery scarf, who bustled about the kitchen.

"*Salaam*, khanum," I said politely.

The woman turned round and peered into my face, a ladle in her hand. Tufts of grizzled hair had escaped from under her scarf, falling on her temples.

"*Thalaam*, Hamid *jaan*!" she cried out in her feeble voice and began to sob. "Why didn't you tell me about your mother and brother?"

I recognised Batool's face, noticeably thinner and pinched-looking, appearing from beyond the dust of years. She walked towards me and hugged me affectionately, her tears trickling on my neck.

Once again Batool had appeared in the sad sky of our lives, brightening it up. From that day on, every Thursday we impatiently awaited the familiar knock on the door.

The Count of Monte Cristo

He would appear from nowhere in the lane as unexpectedly as he would disappear again, like a genie. Whenever I saw him after his long absences, he looked scruffy, his clothes covered in dust and his shoes greasy.

"I think he's a driver's mate who travels to faraway places," one of the neighbours would say.

"He looks more like a smuggler," another neighbour would say another day. "He probably travels to Afghanistan to smuggle in opium."

The neighbours went on with their wild speculations.

"Are you a driver's mate?" I once ventured to ask him.

"Nope," he said, baffled. "Why?"

"Because you suddenly disappear and when you come back your clothes are greasy," I said. He looked at me vacantly and said nothing.

He lived with his mother in a little makeshift hovel the size of a matchbox at the end of the vacant lot choked with garbage beside a garage across our street. They had taken his father to prison long ago. No one ever mentioned what the crime of his father was. The neighbours always talked about him in hushed voices. He came out of prison for a few weeks and then was taken back again for a few years. All the neighbours were used to his comings-out and goings-in. After months of his absence, whenever they saw him shambling towards the grocer's or the baker's, they were not at all taken by surprise and chatted to him as if they had seen him just the day before.

In his sudden disappearances and reappearances, the son had trodden in his father's footsteps. The son, however, seemed quite a sensible young man. No one had ever heard of him committing a petty crime, getting into trouble with anyone, smoking, drinking, chasing the young women, nothing. Everybody was mystified by his sudden disappearances. They nicknamed him 'Greasy Ali' on account of his filthy and greasy clothes.

"Do you know anything about your son's whereabouts when he's not around here?" I asked his mother one day.

"If only I knew, dear," she sighed heavily, "I'd have told you." She then added after a pause: "If he ever speaks to you about where he goes, please let me know and I'll pray for you."

*

One day as I was standing outside the garage smoking and chatting with the owner, I saw Ali's mother shambling along the pavement, fluttering her hands before her. As she approached me I heard her mutter curses, raising her hands to heaven.

"May God give you a long life, dear," she said, planting herself in front of me. "Could you please take me to the police station in Mowlavi Square?

"Police station?" I said, flicking my cigarette butt away.

"Yes, dear," she panted.

"What has he done, Naneh Ali?"

"I don't know," said she. "Half an hour ago a policeman shouted at me to step outside of our hovel. He told me I should at once go to the station. I went in to put on my shoes. When I came out he had gone. As I've seen you talking to my son sometimes, I only thought of you who could take me to the police station.'

I asked my friend if his mechanic lad could drive us there.

"Ohoy, Ahmad," he called out, "jump into my van and drive my friend and Naneh Ali to the police station."

The gate of the police station was mobbed by a throng of people waving papers in their hands. I pushed Naneh Ali through the crowd towards the gate. Upon seeing her, a bad-tempered policeman recognised her and beckoned us to go in. We were led into a room at the end of a short corridor. The lanky swarthy officer who was sitting behind a large desk raised his head and eyed us up and down.

"What's this old woman doing here, Officer Ghanbari?" he asked.

"This is the mother of that young man who hangs around the station some days," Officer Ghanbari said, saluting the captain.

"Oh, yes, yes," the captain muttered. "Sit down, mother." He then turned to Officer Ghanbari and said: "Nip off and bring a glass of water for the old woman."

As Officer Ghanbari was handing the glass of water to Naneh Ali, the captain ordered him to go and fetch Ali. In a few minutes the door opened and Ali walked in, followed by the officer. Dishevelled and filthy, Ali stood there with his hands hanging beside him, gazing mutely at the floor.

“Sit down,” the captain ordered. Ali was staring at me as if wondering why his mother had dragged me along to that place.

“What has he done, Captain?” Naneh Ali asked in a trembling voice.

“He’s done nothing wrong, mother,” grumbled the captain. “He keeps loitering around the station some days from dawn to dusk. I’ve told him several times not to hang around the place. But he doesn’t listen. It’s as if I’m talking to a wall.”

“Be magnanimous and forgive him, Captain,” Naneh Ali whimpered from under her chador. She then got up and grabbed her son’s hand, dragging him from the chair. “Get up,” she said.

Greasy Ali got up like an automaton and followed his mother as if she was his guarantor. The captain looked on silently.

“Let them go, Officer Ghanbari,” I heard the captain say through his moustache, throwing a sidelong glance at the officer.

*

Back in her hovel, Naneh Ali insisted that I should stay and have some tea with them. Seeing Ali’s sullen face, I said goodbye to both of them and decided to leave. I had not gone a few steps that Naneh Ali called out my name. I stopped and looked back. She walked close to me and said: “Could you please tell him son that he won’t get his father back any quicker hanging around the police station.”

"Yes, mother," said I, "I'll talk to him when I see him again." I left her.

The following morning I saw Ali in the lane. Curious as to where he was going, I decided to shadow him. Once out of the lane, he turned right, dragging his feet on the uneven cobblestones of the pavement. I was sure he was heading yet again towards the police station. He seemed so wrapped up in his thoughts, he hardly ever looked back. I kept close to him. After shuffling along the lanes and alleys, he finally arrived at the station. To my surprise, he passed it by without the slightest interest, as if the building was just another ordinary one.

After walking through a small lane, he climbed over a low broken wall beyond which lay a vast garbage dump that was baking under the cruel sun. Once he vanished among the piles of trash, I did the same, threading my way through the rubbish. The stench nearly suffocated me. Ali trudged his way carefully through the piles of garbage as if he knew where he was going. Right at the end of the tip, he entered a makeshift shack made of rusty corrugated tin sheets' and roofed with filthy blue tarpaulins, leaning against the precarious wall of the lot. I hid behind a stack of dented gasoline drums and waited, all the while being eaten up by gigantic gadflies.

It was not long before Ali drew aside the filthy rag that hung from the roof of the shack and emerged carrying a rust-crusted, dented metal chair in one hand and a thick, dog-eared book in the other. He placed the chair beside the shack in the shade, sat on it, and started reading the book. I went on watching him secretly. He was totally lost in his book, not minding the stench or the tormenting gadflies buzzing around him, landing on his face, head, and his book.

As he went on reading, I observed him with curiosity and astonishment. How could this young man manage to concentrate in that hell? What was he reading that had taken up all his attention? Despite the sweltering heat and foul odours around me, I went on watching him. Several times I thought about leaving, but I was not able to tear myself away. I could hear nothing but the humming of obnoxious insects and the distant, muffled hustle and bustle of Tehran.

Ali, all of a sudden, stopped, shut the book and fell into silent contemplation of the slimy ground before him. I looked at my watch. Nearly an hour had passed. He picked up the chair, thrust his book under his arm and disappeared inside the shack. After a minute or two, he stepped outside and walked towards the low wall, deep in thought. No sooner had he climbed over the wall and was lost from view than I dashed to the shack, drew aside the rag and stepped in.

The shack was so small you could not swing a cat in it. A tattered blanket covered with stains was spread on the floor. In one corner stood a rusty-green Aladdin heater, a dented kettle roosting on top of it. Placed beside the heater were a chipped teapot, a tiny tea glass in a saucer, and dirty tin sugar bowl. On the far side I saw, to my bewilderment, a makeshift bookshelf made out of bricks and wooden planks and choked with dozens of books. On the rickety chair beside the shelves lay a large volume. That's the book he was reading outside, I thought. I walked over to the chair and picked the book up. The cover read: *The Count of Monte Cristo*. As I began to examine it, I found a piece of paper used as a bookmark towards the end of the book. "He must've read most it," I mumbled to myself, looking at the books piled on the shelves.

What a cosy little place this young man had created for himself away from that madding crowd outside! Who could ever imagine Greasy Ali would ever read anything, let alone all these books! Upon hearing distant footsteps, I came out of the shack and hid behind the stack of gasoline drums. Greasy Ali was hurrying towards the shack.

From an opening in the stack, I saw him carrying in one hand a paper packet of grapes and a half *sangak* bread in the other. He entered the shack. I was about to come out of my hiding place when I saw Ali come out of the shack, dragging the chair in one hand, the same book tucked under his arm, with a tea glass in the other. He settled in the same spot, opened his book and was plunged at once into reading, sipping his tea from time to time. Once he finished his tea, he sat there, mute and motionless, his eyes fixed on the page. His only movement was when he turned a page. I went on watching him for a while longer.

The yapping of some mongrel dogs made me start. I surveyed the dump that was now shimmering under the harsh midday sun. Three mongrel dogs were fighting over pieces of offal, growling at each other. As the foul smell was beginning to make me nauseous, I decided to leave.

*

I did not see Ali for a whole week. None of the neighbours asked me about his whereabouts. I, however, knew where he was.

A few months later, Ali, like many other young men, was swept away by the hurricane of the Islamic Revolution. Throughout the chaos of the Revolution I visited the shack several times. Everything inside had been looted. It was as if no one had ever lived there. Instead of Ali Greasy, I saw a mongrel bitch lying in the corner of the shack nursing her puppies. As she snarled at me every time I approached, I abandoned the hope of ever finding Ali there.

Grief-stricken, Ali's mother soon passed away almost unnoticed. Some bearded, bear-like men in uniform, dressed in parkas with Kalashnikovs slung over their shoulders, appeared in the lane every so often and took Ali's father to prison, only to let him out after a few months.

After a year they left the father alone. He went on living on his own without talking to anyone. Then he, too, one day vanished without explanation.

Greasy Ali, who had probably uttered no more than one thousand words in his short life, was lost like a wisp of a straw in the bottomless cesspool of our turbulent society for ever without leaving the slightest of traces. I always wondered whether he had any friend or companion in whose mind the memory of him could linger for a while before vanishing altogether.

I kept, however, wondering why he was reading *The Count of Monte Cristo*. What was in that novel that attracted his interest so much? Was it the idea of the injustice done to the protagonist of the novel? The beautiful woman he loved so much? Or the fact that the two young lovers finally found one another and led a happy life?

I wish Greasy Ali, the cultured vagabond, was still there to answer all these questions.

The Search

Whenever we got our leave papers, we thrust them into our uniform pockets and ran, wild with joy, like children scampering out of school at the start of the long summer holidays.

That morning in August, after being handed our papers by the corporal, we trudged through the stretch of barren fields behind the artillery to stand by a dusty road, waiting for a car or a truck to appear to give us lifts to the cities.

With happy thoughts of a week of rest with our relatives in other parts of the country, we belted out bawdy songs, as soldiers on leave do, prancing about like lunatics let out of the madhouse. We then fell to discussing the women in Ahvaz and Khorramshahr, who had lost their breadwinners in the war, and were ready to become our *siegheh*s for an hour or so in order to support themselves and their children.

After an hour of standing under the cruel sun, there was no sign of a vehicle. Worn down by exhaustion and the blinding sun, our enthusiasm began to fizzle out, leaving our hearts as desolate as those lands around us. One by one we fell into gloomy silence, no longer looking at the end of the road, but contemplating our boots. My friends, finding the heat too much to bear, dragged themselves towards a few sickly-looking trees with dusty leaves that stood along a dried-up stream like worn-out pilgrims, and sprawled under their sparse shade as they waited. The sandy bed of a stream snaked up to a faraway hillock, behind which lay a valley, lost amid distant mountains shrouded in a purple-hued haze.

Spurred on by the hope of leaving that hell, I remained beside the road, gazing at the shimmering mirage silently rippling over the arid lands upon which the sun beat, merciless and indifferent as fate itself. I didn't think anyone would be mad enough to come all this way in this inferno to go to Ahvaz or Andimeshk. I looked towards the barrels of the tanks and artilleries on the far edge of that grim wasteland. They resembled long metal spikes stuck out of a shambolic heap of rusted metal, pointing towards deaf-and-dumb heavens from among killing machines abandoned by our routing army. Like reclining ghouls of the desert, slumbering under the relentless sun, the tanks had all fallen silent. One could hear the occasional rumble of enemy artillery fire to which the tanks did not respond, their drivers either having been trapped in them or fled.

From time to time I fixed my gaze at the hillock that obscured the road beyond it. That hillock acted as a sign of hope behind which lurked the fantasy of the sudden appearance of a vehicle that would take us away from that godforsaken place, scorched and laid waste by unbearable heat and constant shelling. How desperately we longed to get out of that graveyard of so many young souls who had been handed gold-plated keys to the gates of paradise by the ayatollahs should they became martyrs in the hope of freeing a wretched patch of our *Islamic* homeland from a barbaric enemy!

I took off my cap and knocked the dust off it by hitting it against my thigh.

Our uniforms were crusted with heavy layers of dust and filth, metamorphosing us into wearied, wandering ghosts of our former selves. Our profuse sweating, having dried out, had left flakes of salt under our armpits. Our worn-out boots, made of shiny black leather when they were given to us, looked like clods of earth, cracked all over and about to crumble any minute and turn into mounds of soil. Two months of non-stop military operations consisting of sorties and retreats had wreaked such havoc on us that we no longer had any sense of our humanity, and were unrecognisable even to one another.

All of a sudden the distant, muffled roar of a motorbike made me jump out of my chaotic reveries. I glanced round at my comrades-in-arms, who sprang up with the agility of goats, scampering towards the road. The motorbike came into view from behind the hillock like a dark patch sliding through the mirage, rattling towards us. As it came closer, I made out a man sitting behind the rider, clinging to him as if for dear life. The motorbike gave a judder and came to a halt in front of us. The man at the back climbed down and strode towards us, clutching his dusty cloth bundle. The motorbike roared off towards the far-off back-up artillery and supplies, its exhaust pipe spluttering black oil on the scorched earth.

Watching the bike lurching away along the road for a while, my friends turned and walked back to the trees, muttering among themselves, disgruntled. I stood beside the road, eyeing the man till he came up to me. He was a tall fellow of about sixty, with heavily wrinkled, sun-burnt skin. His dishevelled grizzly hair, covered with a film of dust mixed with sweat, was stuck to his head. Shining drops slid down his furrowed forehead as red as brick, and over his grey-and-white stubble of a few days. Not in military uniform, he seemed from distant rural parts. He wore a collarless, crinkled white shirt, the neck button of which was tightly fastened. Over his shirt he wore a grey waistcoat. His shabby black jacket was covered with thick dust. His long black trousers gathered over his scruffy *givehs* were also laden with dust. Like an outsider in a remote village, he seemed out-of-place in that war-ravaged region.

"*Salaam,* brother," he greeted me in the dignified manner of a peasant greeting a military man.

"*Salaam*, father," I returned his greeting. "Where are you coming from?"

"From Baneh," he said in the pompous but decent voice of a village headman.

"What were you doing in Baneh?" I asked.

"I'd gone there to see if I could find my son," he said.

"Your son!"

"*Haa*, brother," said he. "He was at the front."

"The front stretches from here to Khorramshahr," I informed him. "Didn't he tell you where exactly he was posted?"

"No," said he. "I haven't heard from him since they took him away from our village."

"Have you been to other places?"

"I've looked for him everywhere," he said. He must have done all he could to find his son.

"What is his name, father?"

"Ramazaan-Ali," said he, digging out a photo from his jacket pocket and handing it over to me. The cracked black-and-white photo showed the pallid skinny face of a young man of about thirty with a shaven head, like that of a newly-conscripted soldier. He was staring with bulging eyes into the void ahead of him. After gazing thoughtfully at the picture a while, I recognised him. His full name was Ramazaan-Ali Baraavi. He had spent some time with me in a trench in the front-line before he was hit on the head by shrapnel from a grenade. He had been *martyred* instantly! Two soldiers had tried to carry him out of the trench. I vividly remember one of them had surreptitiously unclenched Ramazan-Ali's fist and snatched the key-to-paradise. In those days the black-marketeers of the keys-to-paradise, blessed by the ayatollahs, paid a goodly thousand *tomans* for those keys! For a poor soldier from a remote village, each key was the source of considerable fortune. Later on the keys acquired the status of holy relics from the war with Iraq.

"Do you recognise him?" the old man asked, snatching back the photo.

"No, I've never seen him," I said, shaking my head. I looked up at him, shamming ignorance.

The old man shuffled towards one of the bare-branched trees and sat down in its meagre shade, leaning against its trunk and staring at the photo.

I joined him.

"Where's your village, father?" I asked, sitting beside him.

"It's very close to the Iraq border." He shooed away the persistent gadflies.

"What do you do over there?"

"I have a plot of land which I cultivate for wheat," said he. "I'm also the headman of the village, sorting out the squabbles over the sharing of water. I act as go-between in the endless bickering among the villages. Sometimes I arrange marriages for the youth of the village."

"Why are you looking for your son, then?"

"They've decided to marry his intended off to another man."

"Why is that?"

"Because her parents are tired of waiting for him to come back and take her to his home," said he. "The mollah of the village has taken a special interest in her and wants to have another wife."

"Another wife?"

"*Haa baleh.*"

"How many wives has he, then?"

"Three already."

"So he wants to have the fourth one to complete his harem, I suppose," I said. The shadow of a bitter smile flitted across my lips.

We both fell silent for a moment. I looked around. My friends were all stretched out like corpses wrapped up in dusty kilims and left in the shady corner of a graveyard. One could hear only the incessant humming of gadflies.

"Do you reckon it will make a difference if your son comes back to the village?" I broke the silence.

"If he shows up there," said the old man, "her parents might change their minds."

He thrust the photo back into his coat pocket and leaned his head against the trunk of the tree, sunk in thought. He looked so worn-out as he struggled hard to keep his eyes open.

"Have you been to The Prince-Of-The-Martyrs battalion?"

"*Na baba*," he mumbled. "Which direction is it?"

"You should go and stand on the other side of this road," said I, pointing to the road. "If a vehicle stops, tell the driver you want to go to Chamhendi."

"Do you reckon I could find my son there?"

"*Inshallah*, father."

"My knees are giving way," he murmured. "I want to go back. There's no one to look after my family. I only have this son who helped me to till the land and reap the wheat. All my nephews are conscripted to the army to fight this cursed war. My plot is left idle in the sun. It's harvest time and there's no one to help me reap the wheat. I've left my duties as a husband and a headman and have been wandering in these deserts for days…"

"Listen to me, father," said I. "You go there and you'll find him."

"*Haa baba*, right you are," said he. He shaded his eyes with his hand, scanning the lands, baking under the sun.

"What are these lands good for?" He spoke in a dreamy voice.

"For nothing, father," I replied, following his gaze. "They're only good for the powerful of this world to ride around in their deadly machines, annihilating the young men."

"*Haa baleh*," said he, a wry smile brightening up his haggard but handsome face. "You know better, son."

The drone of a coach engine made me start. I looked in the direction of the noise and saw a coach heading our way, raising a cloud of thick dust behind it. I cried out at my drowsing comrades-in-arms to get up. They leapt to their feet, looked around like travellers in ancient times left behind a departed caravan, rubbed their eyes and scrambled towards the road. The bone-shaker, amid a din of clanking metal, came to a halt in front of me. The old man also rose from his place. My friends climbed into the coach, ignoring the old man who hesitated near the door of the coach.

"Go on, father," I said to him, gently urging him to get in. "There are enough seats for everyone."

"No, son," said he. "Let me try The-Prince-Of-The-Martyrs battalion as well. If I don't find my son there, I'll come to Ahvaz to see if I can get some news of his whereabouts."

As he seemed determined to find his son, I bade farewell to him, wishing him good luck. I climbed up into the coach and settled at the back seat. The coach rattled off, leaving the old man behind.

I turned and looked at him, standing forlorn, albeit proud and upright, on the edge of the road, in the manner of a village headman. As the coach moved on, the old man was swallowed up by the thick cloud of dust and was lost from the view.

*

Towards the end of my short leave in Tehran, it was all of a sudden announced, amid a clamour of pomp and ceremony, that the war with Iraq had come to an end. Saddam Hossein had abruptly decided to make peace with the ayatollahs by pulling out of Khorramshahr, giving the patch of land back to them. He needed an ally to fight another war on a different front. The mollahs got to work at once. They scuttled from mosque to mosque like dung-beetles, braying in their ass's voices that *they* had demolished Saddam's army which had fled ignominiously from our *Islamic* country.

Soon the capital city was flooded with thousands of displaced women from the cities in the war zones. Having lost their husbands, sons and brothers, they came to Tehran to get help from the ayatollahs. After a while, cheated and disillusioned, many of them had no choice but to become *siegheh*s to the mollahs and the rich merchants. Once their lustful appetite for cheap sex was gratified, these brutes kicked these wretched women out into the gutters. The women then had to turn to prostitution, wandering like lost souls in purgatory along the main thoroughfare of Tehran's Vali Asr Street, to pick up clients in order to support their kids.

Then came the period in which our nation witnessed the greatest freak show in our history. For months on end, soldiers crippled during eight years of war with Iraq, were paraded in wheelchairs through the streets of Tehran, praised in the controlled media for their sacrifices for the newly-founded Islamic Republic, and honoured and blessed by the supreme religious leader. During longwinded sermons by little and large ayatollahs, these disfigured wretches were told that after they had departed this mean world of ours, their places in paradise would be guaranteed. As foot-soldiers of Islam, they would not have to wander in purgatory for their fate to be determined by Allah. They could speedily bypass the formalities of Judgement Day without being questioned about sins committed in this base life. Once in paradise, the compassionate and merciful Almighty would chuck their artificial limbs down to earth to be used by the living, and make brand new ones made of flesh and blood grow with which they would be able to embrace gorgeous *houris* until eternity.

The only people who profited from all that carnage were the mollahs, the Western powers who sold countless weapons to both countries, and, of course, the merchants who imported millions of artificial limbs to Iran.

*

I often thought about that old man. Did he find the corpse of his son? If so, how did he react? What was he doing in his village, if he were still alive, that is? Was he still sorting out squabbles over irrigation? Was he still presiding over arranged marriages? Or had he simply left this wonderful world?

Glossary

Aladdin: the name of a brand for gasoline heaters used for heating and cooking

baba: literally means 'father'. But it is used as a word of endearment when an older person addresses a child or a younger person.

baleh: yes

chador: Literally means 'tent'. An open black cloak that covers the head and the entire body.

chibouk: A clay pipe with a long stem

giveh: a type of cotton sandals, worn especially in summer in rural central Iran

hauz: An ornamental pond in the middle of courtyard in traditional Persian houses used for washing, floating fruits in them, and ablutions.

houri: a nymph in Paradise

Inshallah: God willing

jaan: dear

joon: dear

korsi: A traditional system of heating in the colder regions of Iran, and some other countries.

Nowruz: Iranian New Year celebrated on the first of Farvardin (21 March)

sangak bread: a type of flat Iranian bread baked on hot pebbles

Shahr-e No: literally 'The Citadel of the New City'. It was the largest brothel in Iran situated in Tehran, enclosed by a wall.

shireh: thickened juice of some fruits, syrup.

siegheh: Under Shiite Law a man may have a maximum of four wives. In addition, he is allowed an unlimited number of temporary wives, who make a marriage contract for a period ranging anywhere from one hour to ninety-nine years. These siegheh wives have no inheritance rights and are not officially registered with the city or the mosque.

ta'zieh: Persian version of Islamic opera re-enacting the death of martyrs who were killed in Karbala along with Imam Hussein during the month of Moharram

tekieh: A temporary mosque.

About the Author

Name: Feridon Rashidi

Biography

Feridon Rashidi was born in Iran in 1955 and came to the UK in 1977. Resident in London, for 28 years he taught in several primary schools in the city. With five degrees from two London University Colleges (B.Sc. Psychology, B.A. French Language and Literature, PGCE, M.Sc. in Child Development, and MA in Theory and Practice of Translation from French to English) he is fluent in Farsi and French. He was a trainee Educational Psychologist for one year. He is now a full-time writer and has written more than 26 short stories, 16 of which are published as a collection, *Tales of Iran*, including the prize-winning story, *Ashura*. The story is also published on *writers'hub.com* and *Iranian.com*. He has also published a mathematics scheme for Key Stage 1 children, *Numeracy Lessons*.

www.ingramcontent.com/pod-product-compliance
Ingram Content Group UK Ltd.
Pitfield, Milton Keynes, MK11 3LW, UK
UKHW041952190726
13854UKWH00005B/1918

9 781785 072802